Master the Scientific Method with Fun Life Science Projects

ANN BENBOW AND COLIN MABLY

ILLUSTRATIONS BY TOM LABAFF

Enslow Elementary

an imprint of

Enslow Publishers, Inc.

40 Industrial Road
Box 398
Berkeley Heights, NJ 07922
USA

http://www.enslow.com

Enslow Elementary, an imprint of Enslow Publishers, Inc.

Enslow Elementary® is a registered trademark of Enslow Publishers, Inc.

Library of Congress Cataloging-in-Publication Data

Benbow, Ann.
    Master the scientific method with fun life science projects / Ann Benbow and Colin Mably.
      p. cm. — (Real life science experiments)
    Includes bibliographical references and index.
    Summary: "Provides an introduction to the scientific method for young readers, using easy-to-do experiments about life science"—Provided by publisher.
    ISBN 978-0-7660-3151-7
    ISBN-10: 0-7660-3148-9
    1. Biology projects—Juvenile literature. 2. Life sciences—Experiments—Juvenile literature. 3. Science—Methodology—Juvenile literature. I. Mably, Colin. II. Title.
    QH316.5.B4 2010
    507.8—dc22
                                  2009019376

Printed in the United States of America

10 9 8 7 6 5 4 3 2 1

♻ Enslow Publishers, Inc., is committed to printing our books on recycled paper. The paper in every book contains 10% to 30% post-consumer waste (PCW). The cover board on the outside of each book contains 100% PCW. Our goal is to do our part to help young people and the environment too!

Illustration Credits: Tom LaBaff

Photo Credits: Associated Press, p. 29; Enslow Publishers, Inc., p. 37; © Mark Evans/iStockphoto.com, p. 25; © Nancy Nehring/iStockphoto.com, p. 12; NASA, p. 13; NASA-JPL, p. 41; Shutterstock, pp. 9, 17, 21, 33; © Tom Hahn/iStockphoto.com, p. 45.

Cover Photo: Shutterstock

Contents

Experiments with a 🏅 symbol feature **Ideas for Your Science Fair.**

Introduction

You have probably asked questions about things you have seen around you. Scientists ask questions about the world, too. They set up tests or experiments to find answers to their questions.

Before beginning an experiment, scientists make predictions about what might happen. They make the predictions based on their knowledge about things that have happened in the past. This prediction is sometimes put in the form of a hypothesis.

To test their predictions, scientists make observations and measurements. These are called data, and are collected using the senses, as well as many kinds of scientific tools. Once data are collected, scientists organize them and look for patterns and relationships. They come to a conclusion based on evidence from the data. Finally, they tell other scientists the results, and think of new questions to investigate.

Science Fair Ideas

The investigations in this book will help you learn the methods that scientists use. After every investigation, you will find ideas for science fair projects. You may want to try one of these ideas, or you might think of a different project.

This book has a Learn More section. The books and Web sites in this section can give you more ideas for science fair projects.

Remember, science is all about asking questions. A science fair allows you to investigate your own questions, record your results in your science notebook, and share your findings with your fellow scientists.

Safety First!

These are important rules to follow as you experiment.

1 Always have an adult nearby when doing experiments.

2 Follow instructions with care, especially safety warnings.

3 Never experiment with electrical outlets.

4 Use safety scissors, and have an adult handle any sharp objects.

5 Use only alcohol thermometers, never mercury!

6 Stay in a safe place if making outdoor observations.

7 Treat living things with care. Some may sting or be poisonous!

8 Keep your work area clean and organized.

9 Clean up and put materials away when you are done.

10 Always wash your hands when you are finished.

Experiment 1
Coming Up With a Question

Question

What questions can you investigate about your pet's behavior? Make a **prediction** and write it in your science notebook.

The first step in any scientific investigation is coming up with a **testable question**. This is a question that lets you investigate only one thing, or variable, at a time. You change just that one variable and keep everything else in the investigation exactly the same. In this investigation, you will be coming up with a testable question about how a pet behaves.

Procedure

1 Observe your pet's eating, sleeping, and playing habits

Things You Will Need

an adult

pet (cat, dog, bird, mouse, hamster, etc.)

pet food dish and food

pet bed or other possession (rug, blanket)

notebook and pen

for one or two days. Record what the pet does. Talk with an adult about questions you could investigate about the pet's habits. What question could you ask about the pet's food, for example? How about where the pet sleeps? Here is one example: "What will happen if I change my pet's brand of food?"

2 Think about how you will test your question. What things do you change in the pet's habits and what do you keep the same? If you were testing the question in Step 1, you might change the pet's usual food to another brand of food. Scientific tests must be accurate and fair. Running the test more than once gives you a chance to make more observations and see if you get the same results each time. This is called **replicating** the test, and makes it fair.

3 Would it be a fair test if you change your pet's food AND where you feed your pet? It is important to only change one thing in a fair test. Choose your question and work with an adult to test it.

Results

Coming up with a testable question is a very special skill in science. It is important that the question lets the scientist test just one thing at a time and keep everything else the same.

Ideas for Your Science Fair

- What testable question would let you know if your reactions were faster than a friend's?

- What testable question would let you know which of two plants needs more water?

- Which testable question would help you to find out which fingerprint pattern is most common in your family?

FACT: Sometimes questions take a long time to test. Gregor Mendel, a monk living in the 1800s, took seven years to finish his research on almost 30,000 pea plants!

Experiment 2
Making Observations

Question

What lives under stones and logs? Make a **prediction** and write it in your science notebook.

An **observation** is something you can see or measure. When you experiment, you need to make **scientific observations**.

You can make observations by using just your senses. Sometimes you can make more accurate observations using tools like cameras, magnifying glasses, and thermometers.

Things You Will Need

an adult

outside area with large stones or log

gloves

magnifying glass

camera

thermometer

notebook and pen

Procedure

1 With your tools, notebook, and pen, go outdoors with **an adult**. Find an area where there are rocks or logs that have been in place for a while.

2 Look carefully at the ground around the rock or log with your eyes and magnifying glass. Is it wet or dry? Measure the air temperature. Take a picture with your camera. Record all your observations.

3 Your adult partner should wear gloves as he or she gently turns over the stone or log. Observe what living things are there, using both your eyes and your magnifying glass. Make notes on what you see in your science notebook. Take a picture, and use the thermometer to see if the temperature is the same under the stone or log as outside. Record the temperature in your science notebook.

4 When you are finished, your adult partner should carefully put the stone or log back into place. Print your pictures and add them to your notebook. The observations that you wrote in your notebook, your photos, and your recorded temperature measurements are your data.

Results

You may have observed that it was darker and cooler under the stone than outside (if the day was warm and sunny). It is often damp under stones and logs, so the living things that you find there must be suited to these conditions. You could have taken pictures of isopods (also called pill bugs or

Isopods live in damp habitats.

sow bugs) in this habitat. Using your magnifying glass, you could observe that they have many short legs, are gray, and curl up in a ball. Other things you may have seen are fungi, earthworms, salamanders, and insect larvae. Using your senses combined with tools gives a good set of data.

 ## Ideas for Your Science Fair

- What kinds of observations tell you whether a habitat is wet or dry?

- What kinds of observations tell you the types of seeds that local birds like best?

- What observations can tell you which eye you favor over the other?

FACT: Scientists use many different kinds of tools. The Hubble Space Telescope orbits Earth. It allows scientists to observe the universe in a way that is not possible from Earth's surface.

Experiment 3
Making Predictions

Question

Is it possible for plants to grow well in just water? Make a **prediction** and write it in your science notebook.

Scientists use their past experiments and knowledge to **make predictions**. Sometimes their predictions are correct, but not always! When predictions are incorrect, scientists try to find out why. They usually do more experiments. Making predictions helps scientists to focus their experiments on exactly what they want to find out.

Things You Will Need

an adult

4 similar petunia plants

4 16-ounce plastic containers with plastic lids

scissors with pointed ends

potting soil

distilled water

metric ruler

measuring cup

notebook and pen

Procedure

1 **Ask an adult** to carefully cut a 3-cm (about a 1-inch) hole in two plastic lids and

a 2-cm hole in the bottoms of two of the containers.

2 Put potting soil in the two containers with holes. Plant a petunia in each one. Put these containers on top of the plastic lids with no holes. Next, put distilled water in the containers with no holes. Fill the water all the way to the top. Cover these with the lids with the 3-cm holes.

3 Wash the soil off the roots of two more petunia plants. Push the roots through the holes in the lids. The plants' roots should be in the water, with their stems and leaves above each of the lids.

4 Use the measuring cup to put equal amounts of water in the containers with potting soil so that the soil is just moist. Put all four cups in a sunny spot. Observe the

plants for two weeks, watering the "potting soil plants" when the soil feels dry, and the "water-only plants" as needed. Record your observations about how well the plants are growing.

5 What did the petunias look like after two weeks? Was your prediction correct? If not, can you explain the difference?

Results

Your prediction for this experiment may have been that petunias need soil AND water to grow. In this experiment, you probably saw that the plants in just water did not grow as well

as the plants in soil. They did not have all the nutrients they needed. Your prediction would have been correct.

 ## Ideas for Your Science Fair

- Will plants grow in salt water as well as in freshwater? Make a prediction and give your reasons.

- What will happen if you hold your nose when you are tasting something? Make a prediction and give your reasons.

- Will frozen seeds sprout as quickly as room temperature seeds? Make a prediction.

FACT: Sometimes when predictions are wrong, it turns out to be a good thing. Teflon™ coating was invented by mistake, and so was the glue for Post-it™ notes!

Experiment 4
Designing Fair Scientific Tests

Question

Yeast feeds on sugar water. What happens to yeast in different temperatures of sugar water? Make a **prediction** and write it in your science notebook.

Every experiment should be a **fair test**. That means that the question must be able to be tested. Also, only one thing can be different between the groups being tested. For this experiment, the water temperature is the ONLY thing that will be different between the two groups. One bowl will have warm water and one will have cold. This way, if there is a difference in how the yeast grows, you can be fairly sure it is due to the different temperatures of the water.

Things You Will Need

- 2 packets of active dry yeast
- 2 quart-size bowls
- 2 teaspoons of sugar
- 2 spoons
- thermometer
- water
- measuring cup
- notebook and pen

18

Procedure

1 Put one cup of warm water in one bowl. Put one cup of very cold water in a second bowl. Take the temperature of the water in each bowl. Record them in your notebook.

2 Add one level teaspoon of sugar to each bowl and stir. Then sprinkle one package of yeast into each bowl, dumping the packets at the same time. Stir again, using one spoon in each bowl.

3 Observe what happens to the living yeast in each bowl. Watch for clouds of yeast to form on the surface, or "bloom." In which bowl does the yeast bloom first? What can you conclude about the best temperature for yeast to grow? Repeat this test twice to check if the result is always the same.

Results

Did you notice a difference in the speed at which the yeast bloomed? You used the same amount of yeast, sugar, and water. The only thing you changed in the test was the temperature of the water. If you noticed a difference, you can say that the yeast bloomed at different speeds because of the water temperature.

Ideas for Your Science Fair

- Design a fair test to show if yeast will grow in both freshwater and salt water.

- Design a fair test to show if your sense of taste is tied to your sense of smell.

- Design a fair test to see which type of seed a certain kind of bird prefers.

FACT: Scientists use people in fair tests when they study diseases. These "clinical trials" help scientists find cures and treatments for many diseases.

Experiment 5
Controlling Variables

Question

Do plants grow toward light or away from light? Make a **prediction** and write it in your science notebook.

Variables are the parts of an experiment that you either change or keep the same. In this experiment, you will be using four of the same kind of plant. Plant type is one variable to control. You will also give the plants the same amount of water and grow them in the same kind of soil. The only variable you will change is the amount of light each plant gets.

Things You Will Need

4 potted bean plants, about 20 cm tall

metric ruler

closet with a door

water

measuring cup

windowsill

notebook and pen

Procedure

1 Look carefully at your bean plants. In what direction are the stems growing? Write down your observations.

2 Make sure that all four plants start out with the same amount of water (the soil should be moist). Put two plants on the windowsill and the other two in the closet. Leave the closet door open about 3 cm (a little more than an inch). What do you think will happen to the plants? Write down your prediction.

3 Every day for two weeks, observe the plants. Write down your observations about the direction the stems are growing and the color of the leaves. Use a measuring cup to make sure that all the plants get watered in exactly the same way. That means you are "controlling the variable" of water amount.

4 After two weeks, what has happened to the stems and leaves of each set of plants? Did this fit with your prediction?

Results

Plants need light to make their own food. They have chemicals in them that cause them to grow toward the light. As you probably saw with your experiment, the stems and leaves of the bean plants in the closet ended up facing the little bit of light that came in through the door. The plants on the windowsill may have also grown toward the light. Since you controlled the variables (kept them all the same) of plant type, soil type, and water, you were able to make conclusions about plants growing toward light.

Ideas for Your Science Fair

- When you want to find out if earthworms are attracted to light, what variables do you have to control?

- What variables do you need to control when you are trying to see which type of food goldfish prefer?

- When you want to test which type of soil is best for growing carrots, what variables do you have to control?

FACT: Controlling variables can even be important in sports. In some forms of motor racing, all the drivers have the same car and are on the same track. What isn't controlled is the drivers' talent to race!

Experiment 6
Collecting Data in Different Ways

Question

How does exercise affect the body? Make a **prediction** and write it in your science notebook.

You can use different methods to **collect data**. To see the effects of exercise on the body, you may decide to take your partner's pulse and record the body temperature using the warmth of his or her forehead. But there are other ways to collect these data. You could use a pulse meter and a thermometer to take the pulse and temperature.

Things You Will Need

a partner
stopwatch
notebook and pen
thermometer (optional)

Procedure

1 This experiment is designed to find out how exercise affects the body. Before you begin, talk with **an adult** about ways of recording what happens when a person jogs in place for two minutes.

26

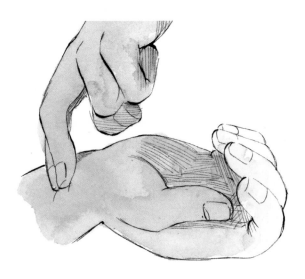

Should you take his or her heart rate, feel his or her skin, or take his or her temperature? Should you take notes, take photographs, draw pictures, or use a combination? Decide on your plan before you begin.

2 Carry out your plan, first with you, and then with your partner. Record your data in your notebook. What did you find out about how exercise affects the body?

3 Now, try another way of recording the effect of exercise on the body. For example, if you took notes the first time, try photographs or pictures this time. Which helped you to learn more about the effect of exercise on the body? Why do you think this was so?

Results

There are many ways to collect data from an experiment. Scientists usually keep a notebook and write down their observations in words and numbers. Field biologists often make drawings of living things, too. It is important to record as many observations as possible during an experiment. You may not realize that a certain observation is meaningful until you have completed your experiment. Since things can happen so quickly in nature, many scientists also record observations with photographs and video.

Ideas for Your Science Fair

- What is the best way of recording how goldfish behave when you bring food to them?

- What would be the best way of recording how a pond habitat changes over time?

- What would be a good way of comparing warning sounds that different birds make?

FACT: Dr. Jane Goodall used a variety of data collection methods in her work with chimpanzees in Africa. Her notes, photographs, and video over many years have helped humans to understand these animals better.

Experiment 7
Organizing Your Data

Question

Which eye color is most common in your family and friends? Make a **prediction** and write it in your science notebook.

The observations you make in an experiment are called **data**. There are different ways of organizing data so that you can see patterns. You can make a list or table, take photographs, or do a combination of these things.

Procedure

1 How will you record eye color so that it is easy to find patterns? When you have decided, set up your notebook to collect the data.

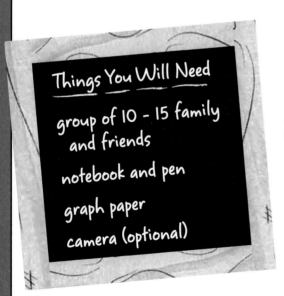

Things You Will Need

group of 10 - 15 family and friends

notebook and pen

graph paper

camera (optional)

2 Look closely at the eyes of your human test group. Record the information in the way you have decided. One way is to use a table.

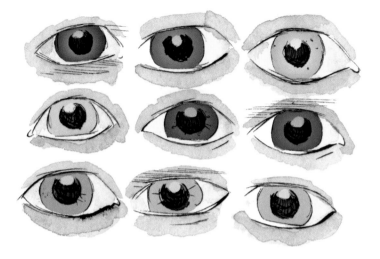

When you finish, choose a method to display your data. You can make a bar graph showing the numbers of friends with a certain eye color.

3 To make a bar graph, draw a chart on graph paper with the numbers of people on the vertical line. Put eye color on the horizontal line. The bar for each color should go up to the number of people in your sample with that color.

4 How many in your sample have blue eyes? Brown eyes? What other eye colors did you observe? What was the most common color of eyes among the people in your sample?

Results

People inherit their eye color from their parents. Brown is the most common eye color in the world, and gray is the least common. By making a bar graph of your observations, you can clearly show which color is most and least common among your friends and family. You may find in your group of friends that blue is the most common color. It all depends on the sample of people you choose to observe.

Table

Bar Graph

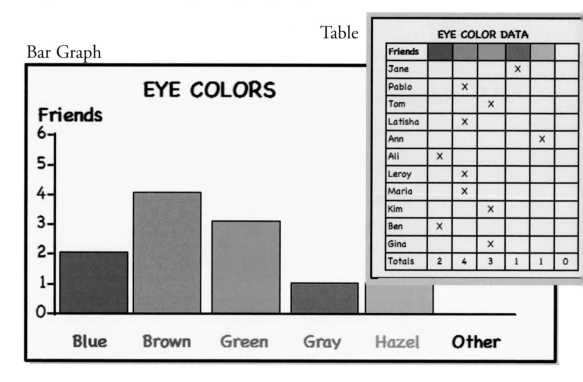

Friends						
Jane				X		
Pablo		X				
Tom			X			
Latisha		X				
Ann					X	
Ali	X					
Leroy		X				
Maria		X				
Kim			X			
Ben	X					
Gina			X			
Totals	2	4	3	1	1	0

Ideas for Your Science Fair

- What kind of table would you use to organize observations about which food goldfish prefer?

- How can you organize weekly photographs showing how a habitat changes over time?

- What kind of table would you use to organize the heights of all the boys and girls in your class?

FACT: Data displays can help scientists and others reach important conclusions. To design complex buildings, architects use scientific data to construct 3D computer models to test their ideas and make sure the structures are strong.

Experiment 8
Finding Patterns in Your Data

Procedure

Do larger seeds make taller sprouts? Make a **prediction** and write it in your science notebook.

Things You Will Need

- packets of seeds (squash, grass, and radishes)
- six 8-oz foam cups
- 6 small plastic plates
- potting soil
- tablespoon
- marking pencil
- water
- graph paper
- colored pencils
- metric ruler
- notebook and pen

Scientists use graphs to show **patterns** in their data. Let's do an experiment to collect some data that you can graph.

Procedure

1 Using a pencil, punch four small holes into the bottoms of six 8-oz foam cups. Fill the cups to within 2 cm of the top with potting soil. Label each cup for the type of seed you will plant in it. (You will plant squash in two, grass in two, and radishes in two.)

34

2 Read each seed packet to find out how deeply to plant the seeds in the soil. Plant three seeds of the same type in each cup. Put a plastic plate under each cup to catch any water that comes out. Sprinkle two tablespoons of water over each cup of seeds.

3 Place the cups and plates in a sunny indoor area. Each day, feel the soil. If it feels dry, add 2 tablespoons of water to each cup. Record the date and the amount of water you add.

4 Using graph paper, make a line graph showing the height of each type of plant over the two-week period (like the one shown on page 36). Use a different colored line for each type of plant.

35

5 Which plant grew the highest? How could you use a bar graph to show patterns in your plant data?

Results

Your graph showed which plants grew the most over time. Not all plants grow at the same rate. One reason is that there are chemicals inside the plants that control growth. Also, plants do not grow as quickly if they do not have enough water, sunlight, or the right soil. Grass usually grows very quickly, radishes a little more slowly, and

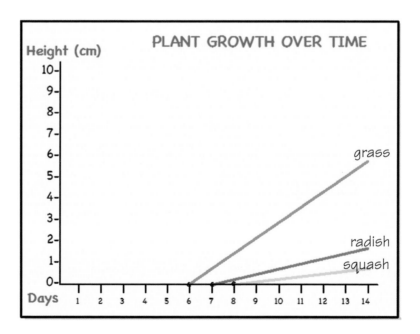

squash is most likely to grow slowest of all. The graph of your data should have showed you that pattern.

 ## Ideas for Your Science Fair

- How can you use a bar graph to show the pattern of different hair colors in your class?

- How can you use a line graph to show how exercise changes your heart rate?

- How can you make a table to help you find out if fingernails grow faster than toenails?

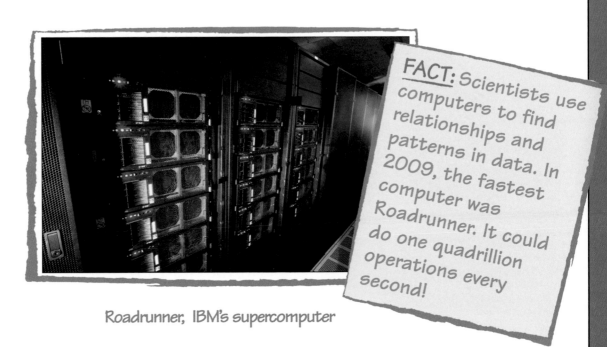

Roadrunner, IBM's supercomputer

FACT: Scientists use computers to find relationships and patterns in data. In 2009, the fastest computer was Roadrunner. It could do one quadrillion operations every second!

Experiment 9
Making Conclusions

Question

Do leaves affect water movement in a plant? Make a **prediction** and write it in your science notebook.

A **conclusion** is a scientist's answer to an experimental question. A scientist makes a conclusion after looking for patterns in the collected data. Sometimes the conclusion matches the prediction, and other times it does not. When the conclusion does not match the prediction, the scientist will usually repeat the investigation.

Things You Will Need

an adult

2 stalks of celery with leaves both the same height

red food coloring

water

2 clear plastic cups

knife

notebook and pen

Procedure

1 Look carefully at the celery stalks. How do you think water gets from the base of the stalk to the leaves? You will be putting the celery stalks into red water and watching to see what happens

to the stalks. One of your stalks will have leaves, and the other will not. Ask an adult to cut 1 cm of the end of each stalk.

2 Fill the two plastic cups ¾ full with water. Add four drops of red food coloring to each cup. Take the leaves off one of the stalks of celery. Put a stalk of celery into each of the cups and leave them overnight in a cool place. What do you think will happen and why?

3 The next day, observe your celery stalks. What happened to the celery in each of the cups? How do you think this happened? How was the celery with the leaves different from the one without the leaves? What can you conclude about the job of the celery leaves? What observations support your conclusion?

Results

At the end of fair tests, scientists look for patterns in their data. These patterns help scientists come up with an answer, or conclusion. In the celery investigation, you could conclude that the leaves play a role in moving the colored water up the celery stalk, since the only difference in your experiment was the leaves.

Ideas for Your Science Fair

- If you had two kinds of seeds in your bird feeder, and all of one kind disappeared first, what could you conclude about your local birds?

- If you took an aquarium plant out of water, and it shriveled up in one day, what could you conclude about what the plant needs?

- If bean seeds that you soaked in water sprouted more quickly that bean seeds you did not soak, what could you conclude?

Mars Phoenix Lander

FACT: New evidence can change earlier conclusions. Scientists thought that Mars had no water. We now know that Mars has water. NASA's Mars Phoenix Lander found traces of water in Martian soil in 2008.

Experiment 10
Communicating Your Findings

Question

How do different habitats in your area change over two seasons? Make a **prediction** and write it in your science notebook.

At the end of this investigation, you will need to find a way to share your results. It is important that you **communicate** several things to others:

Things You Will Need

outdoor area with plant life

thermometer

camera (optional)

poster-making materials

computer with PowerPoint (optional)

notebook and pen

- Your investigation question
- What you did to investigate the question (procedure)
- Your data and results
- Your conclusions

Procedure

1 This investigation takes a long time. Choose an area in your backyard, schoolyard, or nearby park that has lots of plant and animal life.

Spring   Summer

2   If you can, start your observations in the spring and end in early summer. In your notebook, record the date of your first observation and the weather conditions (temperature, cloud cover, precipitation, and windiness).

3   Write down the types of plants and animals you observe in a certain area. If you can, draw this area or take a picture. When you download or print your picture, be sure to label it with the date as well as a name. Continue to make observations and take or draw pictures every two weeks in the same place. Do this for at least three months.

4   At the end of your observations, look over all your data. How did the habitat you observed change from

spring to summer? How did the plants and animals change? Why do you think this happened?

5 When you finish your investigation, use the poster-making materials or the computer to make a display of your results. Be sure to include your pictures as part of your observations. Share this with an adult or friend. Is your presentation clear? If not, ask for suggestions and change your display.

Results

Scientists share their results in many ways. Sometimes they make posters showing their findings and share these at

conferences. Other times, they make computer presentations to share with other scientists. Another way scientists share results is to write articles for scientific journals. In this way, scientists keep adding to the work of other scientists.

 ## Ideas for Your Science Fair

- How can you best communicate the results of a fingerprint survey of your classmates?

- What is a clear way of communicating which plants are able to grow in just water?

- How can you use a poster to communicate how living things come back to a bare patch of ground?

Mesopotamian clay tablet

FACT: Some of the earliest scientific results that were shared were on clay tablets from Mesopotamia from about 500 B.C. Think of how different it is today, when scientists can share information in seconds via the Internet.

Words to Know

biologist—A scientist who studies living things.

communicate—To share information with others.

conclusion—An answer to a scientific question.

data—Observations and measurements.

evidence—Data that support a conclusion.

fair test—An investigation in which only one variable changes at a time.

findings—The results from a fair test.

graphing—A way of showing patterns in data.

habitat—A place in which an organism lives.

larvae—Insects at the early stage of their growth.

nutrients—Chemicals that organisms need to thrive.

observation(s)—Information collected through the senses.

organism—A living thing.

prediction—An expected result of a fair test.

procedure—The method of testing a scientific question.

replicating—Repeating a test to check results.

variables—Parts of a test that may be changed or kept the same.

Learn More

Books

Bochinski, Julianne Blair. *The Complete Handbook of Science Fair Projects.* Hoboken, New Jersey: John Wiley & Sons, Inc., 2004.

Rhatigan, Joe, and Rain Newcomb. *Prize-Winning Science Fair Projects for Curious Kids.* New York: Sterling Publishing, 2006.

VanCleave, Janice. *Great Science Project Ideas from Real Kids.* New York: Sterling Publishing Co., Inc., 2006

Internet Addresses

Biology4Kids - Scientific Studies.
http://www.biology4kids.com/files/studies_scimethod.html

Science Experiments For Kids.
http://homeschooling.gomilpitas.com/explore/sci.htm

Scholastic—Let's Investigate.
http://www2.scholastic.com/browse/article.jsp?id=639

Index

DATE DUE

Demco